SCRIPTURAL WAY OF THE CROSS

Fr Adrian Graffy

*All booklets are published
thanks to the generosity of the supporters
of the Catholic Truth Society*

CATHOLIC TRUTH SOCIETY

PUBLISHERS TO THE HOLY SEE

Images courtesy of Fr Adrian Graffy, Catholic Church of Christ the Eternal High Priest, Gidea Park.

Biblical text © Darton, Longman and Todd Ltd 2018. Translated by Dom Henry Wansbrough OSB.

All rights reserved. First published 2020 by The Incorporated Catholic Truth Society, 42-46 Harleyford Road London SE11 5AY Tel: 020 7640 0042 Fax: 020 7640 0046. © 2020 The Incorporated Catholic Truth Society.

ISBN 978 1 78469 627 6

CONTENTS

The Message of Scripture 4

Traditional prayers said at each station 6

Stations of the Cross 9

The Message of Scripture

Catholics have an extraordinary devotion to the Way of the Cross. The fourteen stations trace the journey of Jesus from his condemnation to the burial in the tomb. In recent times a fifteenth station is sometimes added, as it is in our presentation, to commemorate the Resurrection. We thus focus on the whole of the paschal mystery of Christ's death and Resurrection.

Each station begins with a short passage from Scripture. This is the main feature and should be read slowly, with time taken afterwards for quiet reflection. Most of the readings are taken from the gospels, but others are from other books of the Bible and are chosen to assist us with a deeper reflection on the suffering of Christ.

Each passage of Scripture is followed by a short prayer addressed to Jesus and linked to the particular station. An invitation to further prayer concludes each station. It is important that these different parts should be punctuated with silence.

The message of the Scriptures is deep and it is hoped that these readings and prayers will foster our love of the Lord Jesus. The Bible translation used is the *Revised New Jerusalem Bible* (Darton, Longman and Todd, 2019).

The photos are of the Stations of the Cross which hang in the Catholic Church of Christ the Eternal

High Priest, Gidea Park, Essex. They are the work of the Italian sculptor, Nico Venzo, and are a precious gift for meditation. You can pray the stations in your own church, at home, or in other locations suitable for prayer. You are welcome to come and pray the stations in our lovely church too.

Prayers to be said at the beginning and end of each station.

V. (genuflecting) *We adore you, O Christ, and we bless you.*
R. *Because by your Holy Cross you have redeemed the world.*

Our Father. Hail Mary. Glory Be.

*Stabat Mater dolorósa, / Iuxta crucem lacrymósa, / Dum pendébat Fílius.	At the Cross her station keeping, / Stood the mournful Mother weeping, / Close to Jesus to the last
Cuius ánimam geméntem, / Contristátam, et doléntem, / Pertransívit gládius.	Through her heart his sorrow sharing, / All his bitter anguish bearing, / Now at length the sword has passed.
O quam tristis et afflícta / Fuit illa Benedícta / Mater Unigéniti!	Oh how sad and sore distressed / was that mother highly blessed / of the sole begotten One!
Quae moerébat, et dolébat, / Pia mater, dum vidébat / Nati poenas ínclyti.	Christ above in torments hangs; / She beneath beholds the pangs / Of her dying glorious Son.
Quis est homo qui non fleret, / Matrem Christi si vidéret, / In tanto supplício?	Is there one who would not weep, / Whelmed in miseries so deep, / Christ's dear Mother to behold?
Quis non posset contristári, / Christi Matrem contemplári, / Doléntem cum Fílio?	Can the human heart refrain, / From partaking in her pain, / In that Mother's pain untold?
Pro peccátis suae géntis, / Vidit Jesum in torméntis, / Et flagéllis súbditum.	Bruised, derided, cursed, defiled, / She beheld her tender Child, / All with bloody scourges rent.

*Each stanza to be said after each station respectively.

Vidit suum dulcem Natum,	For the sins of his own nation,
Moriéndo desolátum,	Saw him hang in desolation,
Dum emísit spíritum.	Till his spirit forth he sent.
Eia, Mater! fons amóris!	O thou Mother! fount of love!
Me sentíre vim dolóris	Touch my spirit from above.
Fac, ut tecum lúgeam.	Make my heart with yours accord.
Fac ut árdeat cor meum;	Make me feel as you have felt;
In amándo Christum Deum,	Make my soul to glow and melt,
Ut sibi compláceam.	With the love of Christ my Lord.
Sancta Mater! istud agas;	Holy Mother! pierce me through;
Crucifíxi fige plagas,	In my heart each wound renew,
Cordi meo válide.	Of my Saviour crucified.
Tui nati vulneráti,	Let me share with you his pain,
Tam dignáti pro me pati,	Who for all my sins was slain,
Poenas mecum dívide.	Who for me in torments died.
Fac me tecum pie flere,	Let me mingle tears with you,
Crucifíxo condolére,	Mourning him who mourned for me,
Donec ego víxero.	All the days that I may live.
Iuxta crucem tecum stare;	By the cross with you to stay;
Et me tibi sociáre,	There with you to weep and pray,
In planctu desídero.	Is all I ask of you to give.

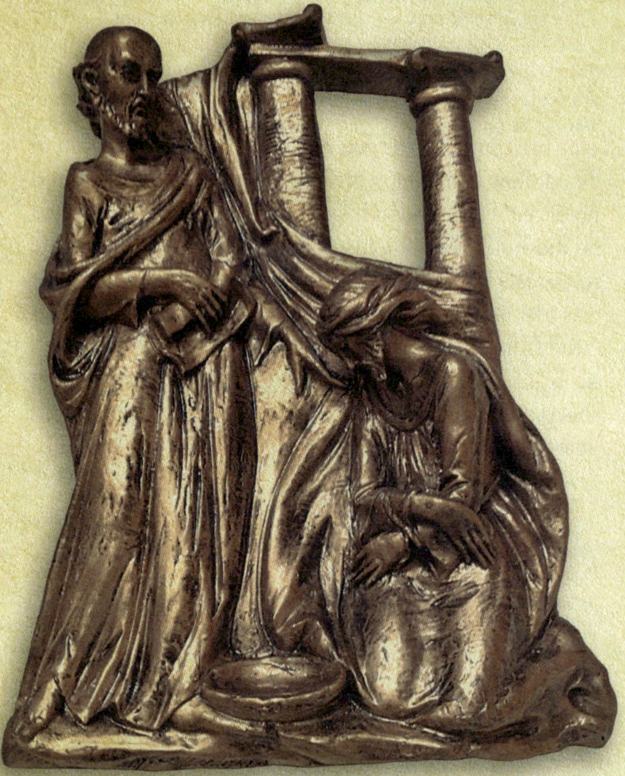

FIRST STATION

Jesus is Condemned to Death

From the First Letter of Peter
(2:21-25)

Christ suffered for you and left an example for you to follow in his steps. He had done nothing wrong, and no deceit was found in his mouth. When he was insulted he did not return the insult, when he suffered he made no threats but put his trust in him who judges justly. He was bearing our sins in his own body on the cross, so that freed from sins we might live for righteousness; through his bruises you have been healed. You were like straying sheep, but now you have returned to the shepherd and guardian of your souls.

PAUSE

Jesus, you have come to the moment which you have long foreseen. You knew that the way of the cross lay before you. Give me strength to bear my cross too.

PAUSE

Pray for those who are condemned to death, and those awaiting execution.
Pray that vengeance will give way to forgiveness in the hearts of all.

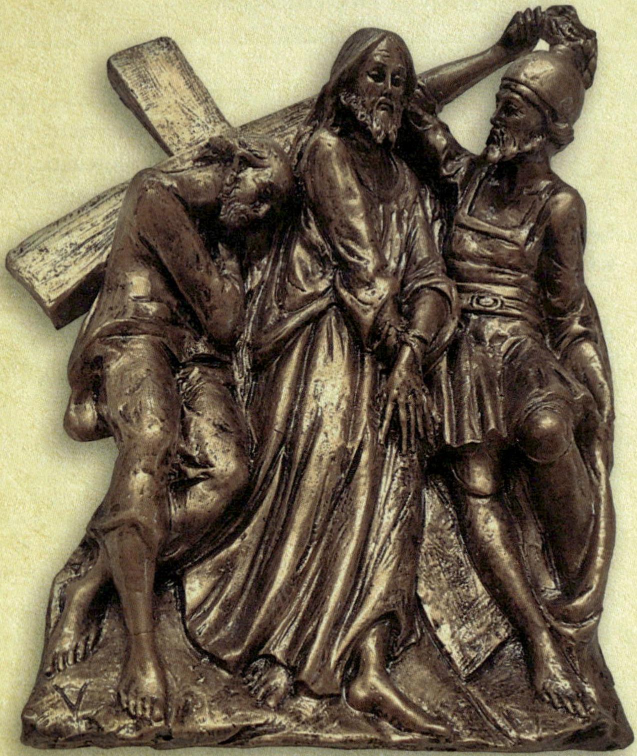
V

SECOND STATION

Jesus Receives the Cross

From the gospel according to Mark
(8:34-35)

Anyone who wants to be a follower of mine must renounce self and take up the cross and follow me. For whoever wants to save life will lose it; but whoever loses life for my sake, and for the sake of the gospel, will save it.

PAUSE

Jesus, your cross is the means of our salvation. Help us to be willing to lose our lives for your sake. Show us the beauty of generosity and self-giving love.

PAUSE

Ask for the grace to give generously and deny self. Welcome the joy of the gospel which no suffering can remove.

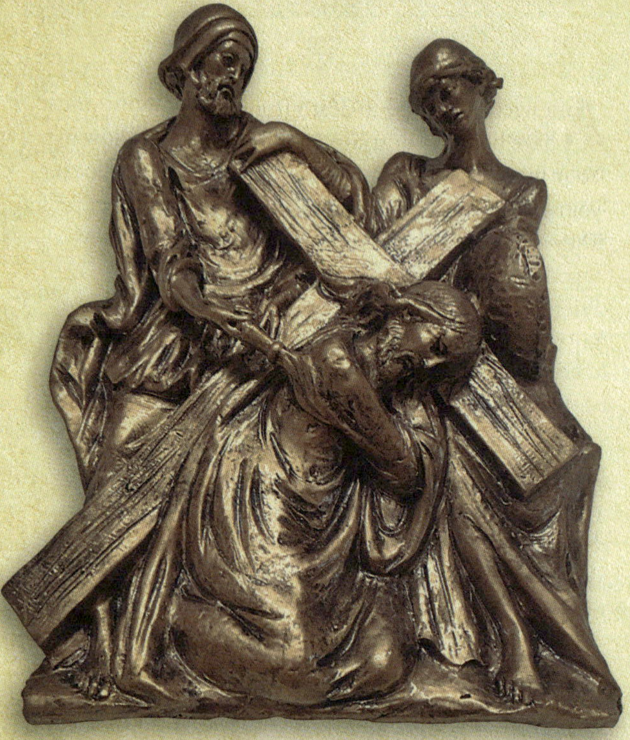

THIRD STATION

Jesus Falls the First Time

From the book of Psalms
(88:16-19)

I am wretched, close to death from my youth.
I have borne your trials; I am numb.
Your fury has swept down upon me;
your terrors have utterly destroyed me.
They surround me all the day like a flood;
together they close in against me.
Friend and neighbour you have taken away:
my one companion is darkness.

PAUSE

Jesus, help me to face the dark times without losing confidence in your nearness to me. When I fall, however I fall, draw me closer to you.

PAUSE

Pray for those in depression and despair, that the light of Christ will penetrate their darkness.

Pray for those who have lost families and homes due to war and violence, that we may assist them to rebuild their lives.

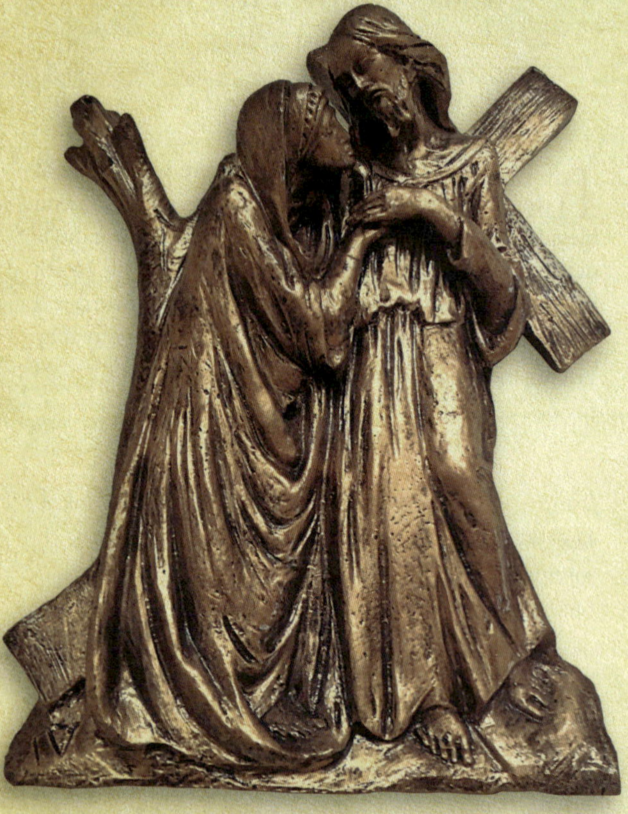

FOURTH STATION

Jesus Meets his Blessed Mother

From the gospel according to Luke
(2:33-35)

As the child's father and mother were wondering at the things that were being said about him, Simeon blessed them and said to Mary his mother, 'Look, he is destined for the fall and for the rise of many in Israel, destined to be a sign that is opposed – and a sword will pierce your soul too – so that the thoughts of many may be laid bare.'

PAUSE

Jesus, your mother was willing to suffer with you. Make us grateful for the ties of love that bind us to the living and the dead.

PAUSE

Pray for a deep attachment to Mary, mother of Jesus, and mother of the Church.
Thank God for the saints of past times, and the saints of today.

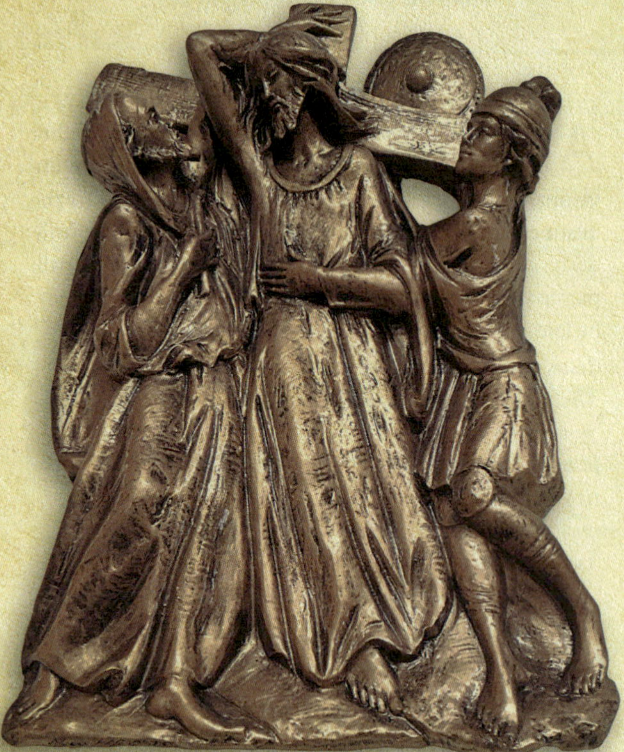

FIFTH STATION

Jesus is Assisted by Simon of Cyrene

From the gospel according to Mark
(15:21-22)

They enlisted a passer-by, Simon of Cyrene, father of Alexander and Rufus, who was coming from the country, to carry his cross. They brought Jesus to the place called Golgotha, which means the place of the skull.

PAUSE

Jesus, brave and good people assisted you on your way. Give courage to all who must stand against tyranny and injustice. Help us to stand up for truth and goodness.

PAUSE

Pray for all who assist others in pain, whether physical, mental or spiritual.

Pray for nurses and doctors, for those who care for the elderly and the dying, for aid workers and those who respond to emergencies.

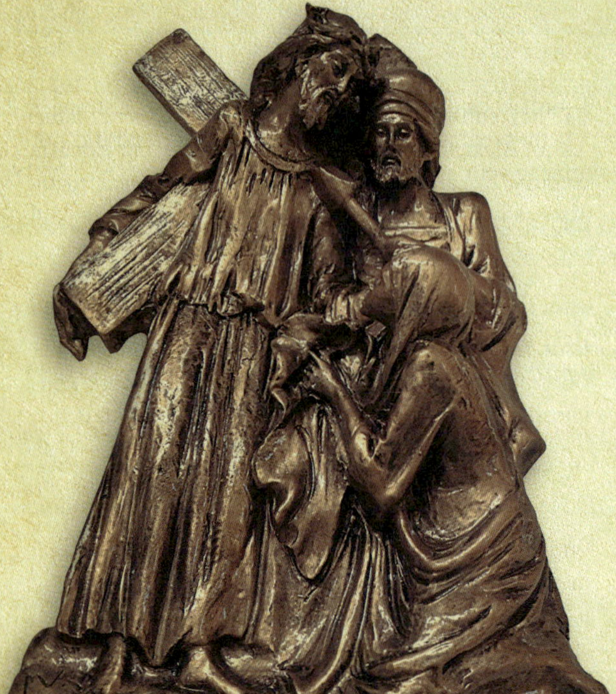

SIXTH STATION

Veronica Wipes the Face of Jesus

From the gospel according to Matthew
(25:44)

L ord, when did we see you hungry or thirsty, a stranger or needing clothes, sick or in prison, and did not come to your aid?

PAUSE

Jesus, the tenderness of Veronica touched your heart. Make us unafraid of showing tender love. Melt whatever is frozen within us, that we too may show mercy.

PAUSE

Pray for a generous heart to share our gifts with the poor.
Pray that the poor will truly be treasured among us.

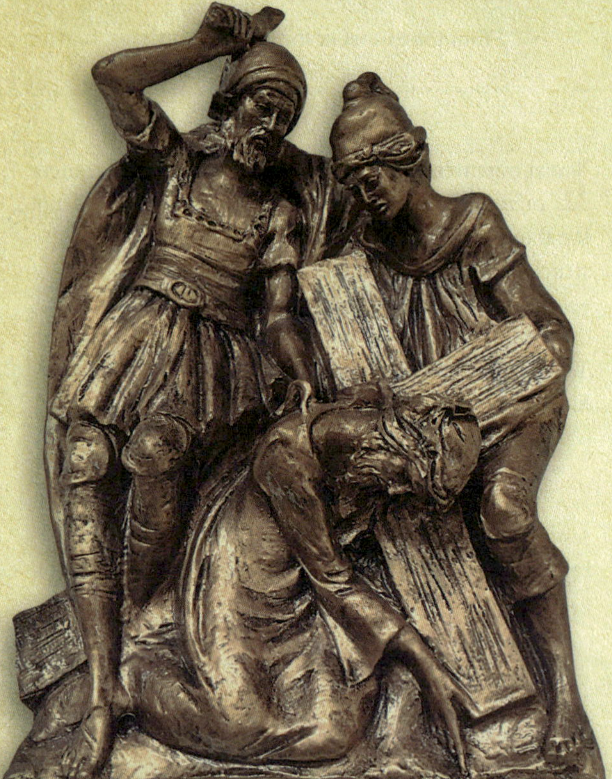

SEVENTH STATION

Jesus Falls the Second Time

From the book of the prophet Isaiah
(53:4-5)

Yet ours were the sufferings he bore,
ours the sorrows he carried.
We thought of him as smitten,
struck down by God and afflicted;
yet he was wounded for our rebellions,
crushed on account of our evil deeds.
The punishment that made us whole was on him:
his wounds brought healing to us.

PAUSE

Jesus, your sufferings are your gift to the world. Help us to see things with your eyes and with your compassion.

PAUSE

Pray for new vision, that we may receive a new heart and a new spirit.
Pray to be free from rigidity and a refusal to change.

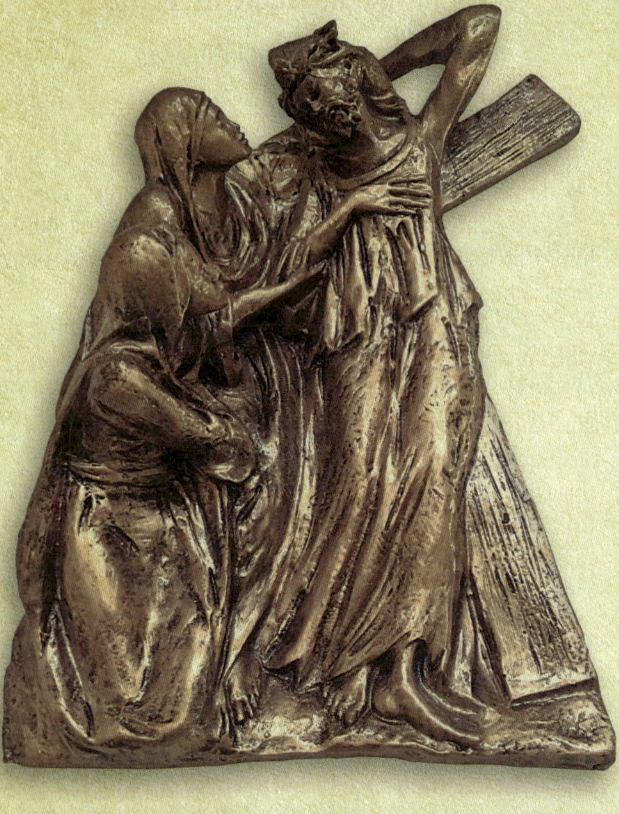

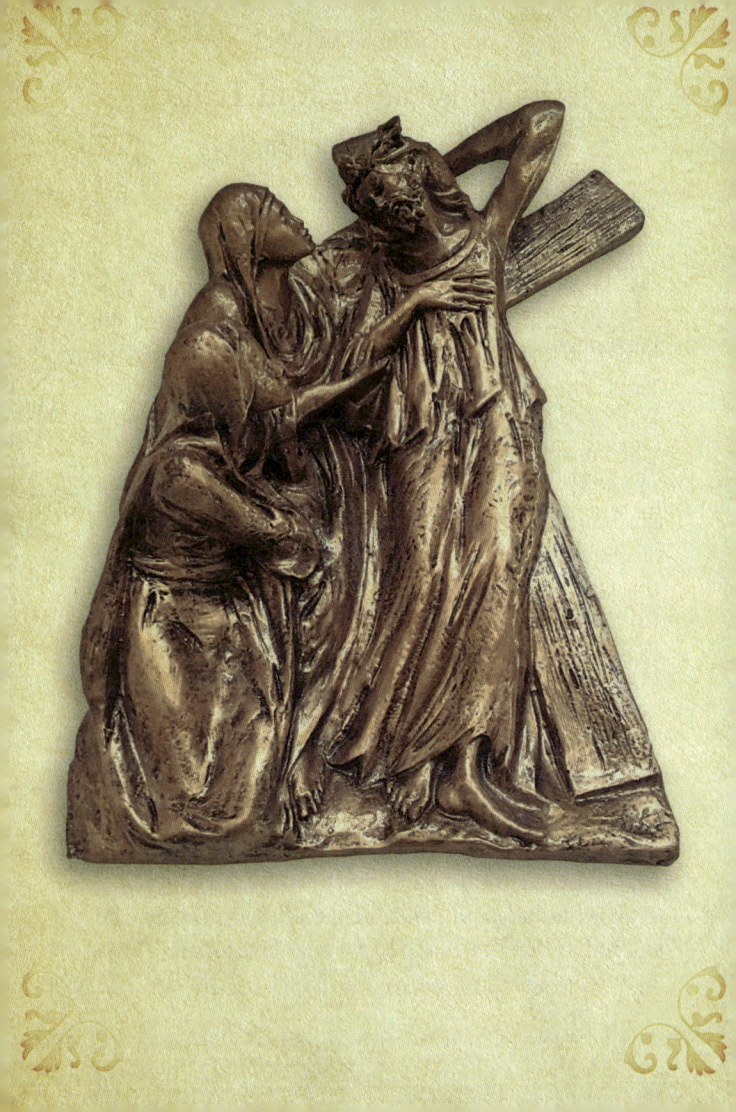

EIGHTH STATION

Jesus Meets the Women of Jerusalem

From the gospel according to Luke
(23:27-32)

A large number of the people followed him, and women, who beat their breasts and mourned for him. But Jesus turned to them and said, 'Daughters of Jerusalem, do not weep for me; but weep for yourselves and for your children. For look, the days are coming when people will say, 'Blessed are the barren, the wombs that have not borne children, the breasts that have not given suck!' Then they will begin to say to the mountains, "Fall on us!"; and to the hills, "Cover us!" For if they do this when the wood is green, what will they do when it is dry?' Two others also, criminals, were led out to be put to death with him.

PAUSE

Jesus, help us to be a light for the people of today. Let us not succumb to despondency and selfishness, but work imaginatively for the good of all.

PAUSE

Pray for leaders and politicians, that their eyes may be opened to true values and to a tender love for all.

Pray for a new spirit of harmony in our society.

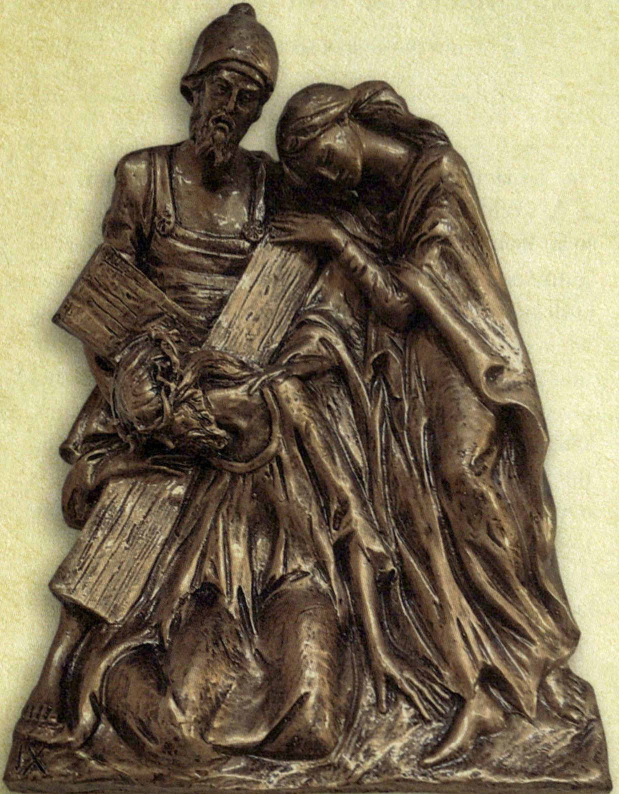

NINTH STATION

Jesus Falls the Third Time

From the book of Psalms
(22:2-3)

My God, my God, why have you forsaken me?
Why is your rescue far from me,
so far from my words of anguish?
O my God, I call by day and you do not answer,
I call by night and I find no relief.

PAUSE

Jesus, your way is hard, your suffering beyond belief.
You persevere with courage and love.

PAUSE

Pray for perseverance in the trials of life, for honesty in prayer, and for acceptance.

Ask for a deeper awareness of God's abiding presence.

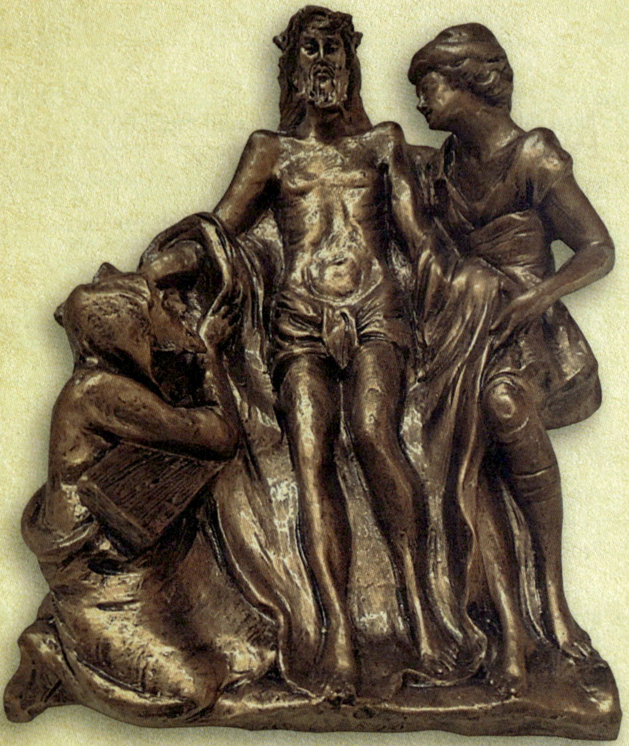

TENTH STATION

Jesus is Stripped of his Garments

From the book of Job
(16:12-14)

I was living at peace until he shattered me,
taking me by the neck to tear me apart.
He has set me up as his target:
his archers surround me, he pitilessly pierces my loins,
and pours my gall out on the ground
Breach after breach he drives through me,
charging on me like a warrior.

PAUSE

Jesus, you share the suffering and pain of your brothers and sisters. You accepted all this for our good. Help us to really know your love.

PAUSE

Pray for the gift of silence, that we may acknowledge God's truth and God's love.
Pray for light in the darkness of this world.

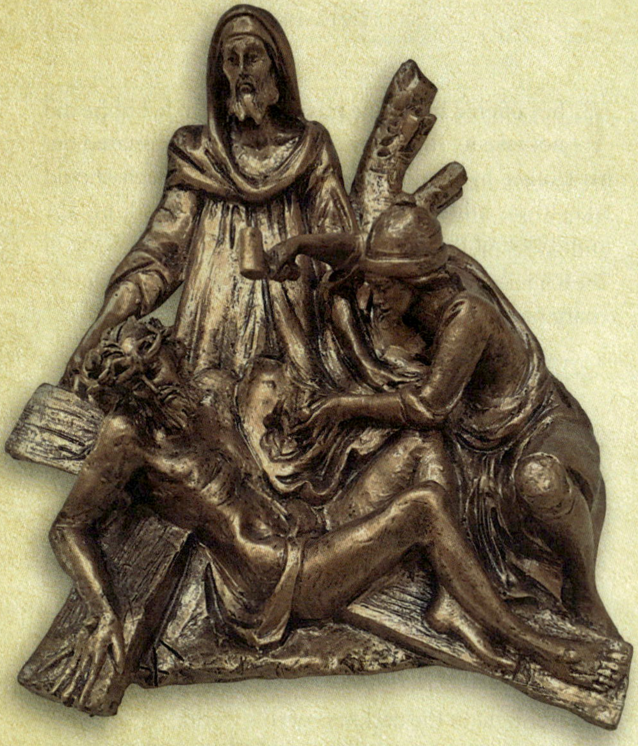

ELEVENTH STATION

Jesus is Nailed to the Cross

From the gospel according to Mark
(15:23-27)

They offered him wine mixed with myrrh, but he did not take it. Then they crucified him, and shared out his clothes by casting lots to decide what each should take. It was mid-morning when they crucified him. The inscription of the charge against him read, 'The King of the Jews'. And they crucified two bandits with him, one on his right and one on his left.

PAUSE

Jesus, you were tortured by your executioners. You stretched out your arms in love in the midst of extreme pain. Can we possibly do the same?

PAUSE

Pray for healing for the sick, and for the abused, that the cross of Christ may inspire us to forgive, and to love as he did.

Help us to give priority to our brothers and sisters in greatest need, and to work together for a better world.

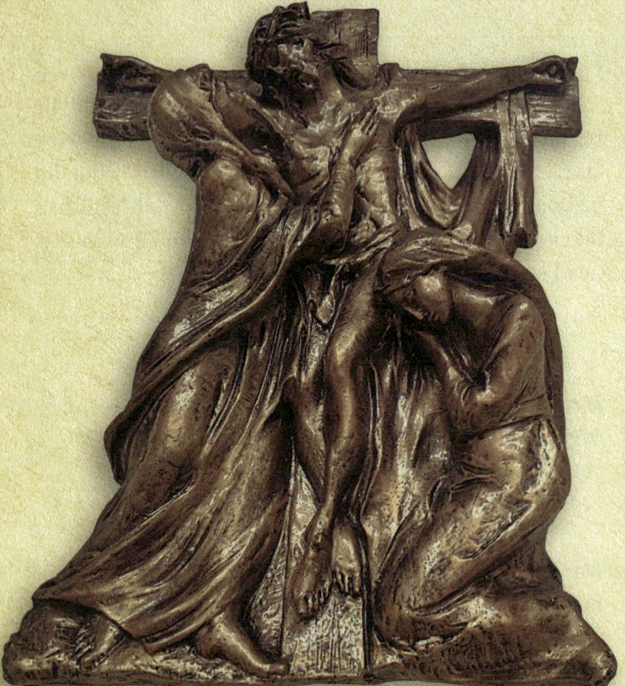

TWELFTH STATION

Jesus Dies on the Cross

From the gospel according to John
(19:28-30)

After this, Jesus knew that everything had now been completed and, so that the scripture should be fulfilled, he said: 'I am thirsty.' A jar full of sour wine stood there; so, putting a sponge soaked in the wine on a hyssop stick, they held it to his mouth. After Jesus had taken the wine he said, 'It is completed'; and bowing his head he gave over his spirit.

PAUSE

Jesus, by your holy cross you have redeemed the world.
We stand in silence at the foot of your cross.

PAUSE

Never forget the power of the death of Christ and of his cross.
Welcome sister Death who leads home the child of God and lights our path.

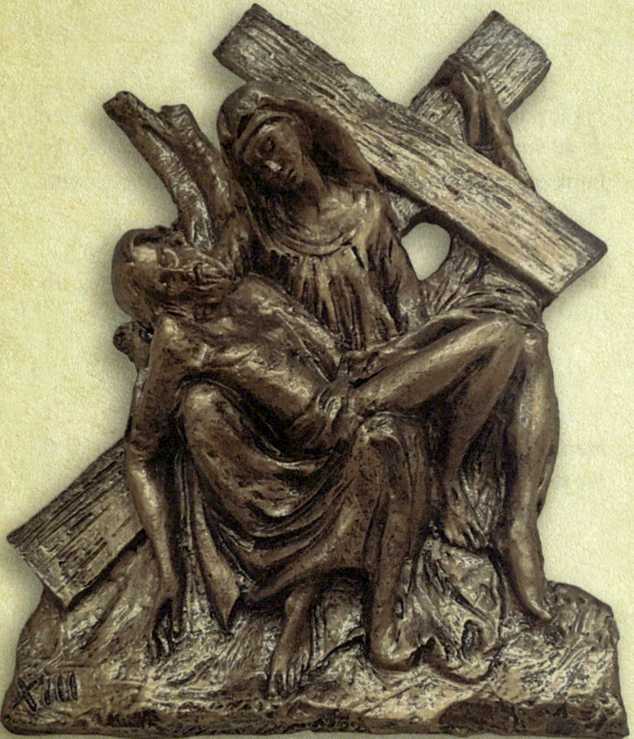
XIII

THIRTEENTH STATION

Jesus is Taken Down from the Cross

From the book of Lamentations
(1:12)

Is it nothing to you,
all you who pass this way?
Look and see if there is any sorrow
like the sorrow brought upon me
which the Lord inflicted
on the day of his burning wrath!

PAUSE

Jesus, your broken body is embraced by your dear mother, Mary. Help us to cradle the suffering and the poor in the brave embrace of mercy.

PAUSE

Pray for those who mourn the loss of loved ones, and for those mourned by no-one.

Thank God for the challenges of faith, the brightness of hope, and the tenderness of love.

XIV

FOURTEENTH STATION

Jesus is Laid in the Tomb

From the gospel according to Mark
(15:42-47)

Now as soon as evening came, since it was Preparation Day – that is, the day before the Sabbath – Joseph of Arimathea, a respected member of the council, who was himself awaiting the kingdom of God, went boldly to Pilate and asked for the body of Jesus. Pilate, surprised that he was already dead, summoned the centurion and asked if he had been long dead. Having been assured of this by the centurion, he granted the corpse to Joseph. Joseph bought a linen cloth, and, taking him down from the cross, wrapped him in the shroud, and laid him in a tomb which had been hewn out of the rock ,and rolled a stone against the doorway of the tomb. Mary of Magdala and Mary the mother of Joset were watching where he was laid.

PAUSE

Jesus, all is silence as you are released from the cross and laid in the tomb. The earth sleeps in peace.

PAUSE

Pray that in silence and in sadness we may come to know God's faithful love.

Be filled with joy in anticipation of the fullness of life in God.

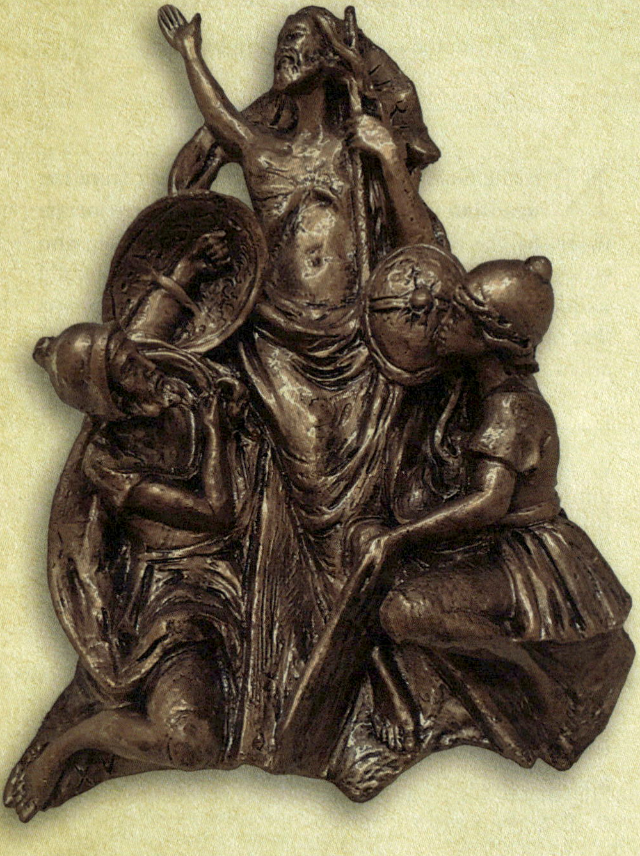

FIFTEENTH STATION

Jesus is Raised From the Dead

From the Letter to the Hebrews
(13:20-21)

May the God of peace, who brought back from the dead our Lord Jesus, the great Shepherd of the sheep, by the blood of the eternal covenant, form you in all good to do his will, effecting in us whatever is acceptable to himself through Jesus Christ, to whom be glory for ever and ever. Amen.

PAUSE

Jesus, risen from the dead you are with us always. Keep the joy of Easter always before us. Let us share this light with everyone.

PAUSE

Celebrate Christ's rising to new life as often as possible in Word and Sacrament.

Look forward to our meeting with him and with our brothers and sisters in the land of the living.